MY CHURCH

House Of God

REV DR Anoweh v.ap

anoweh bigg k

The characters and events portrayed in this book are fictitious. Any similarity to real persons, living or dead, is coincidental and not intended by the author.

ISBN-13:9798351773346

Cover design by: bigg
Printed in the United States of America

This book is dearly dedicated to my immediate family, my Friends and committed members of the body of Christ who are ready to sacrifice all for the sake of our Lord Jesus Christ.

CONTENTS

FOREWORD

I am privileged to be asked to write the foreword of this little but very powerful book. Though much truth is hidden but, revealed between the front and back cover of this religious instructional manual. This book is a revelation of the mind of a shepherd to his flock. I have purposely underlined three words in the first paragraph of this foreword because they represent what I think about Revd, Dr. Anoweh Vitalis and "MY CHURCH"

POWERFUL: Spiritual power I believe does not stem from fire crackers, comet and thunderstorms of great miracles. No! These mercies call for attention. Spiritual power, in the nature and manner of Christ consists of the ability to use simple events and circumstances to make a languishing soul willingly buy into eternal truth and surrender to it. You will find this book powerful because it is going to engage you to the truth you cannot deny as a child of God.

RELIGIOUS INSTRUCTIONAL MANUAL: A manual is made up of series of steps that lead to understanding. Understanding creates confidence in practice and tutorial. A manual is non-ambiguous and leads to positive developments and growth.

"My Church" is such a manual which if you follow it's prescriptions, Will surely experience personal turnaround in Christ and be a blessing (tutor) to others, irrespective of your denomination

THE MIND OF A SHEPHERD: Every servant of Christ, serving in the manner and mind of Christ must be a shepherd, a "gatherer"

and not a “scatterer”. Pastor Anoweh has tried in this book to lure away from fulfilling a prophecy: one of the signs of the second coming of Christ and the end of the age which is that.... “the love of many (for Christ and his church) will grow cold" Matt 24:3 and 12. It will rather help you add one more chord to the inaudible answer to Christ’s very important question: "when the son of man shall return, will he find faith on earth"?

By the time you(youth, father, mother, minister or elder) go through this book, you will discover that outside the community of the faithfuls, the church, you are nowhere hence I strongly recommend this book to you. God bless you.

REV. ONWUKWE, E.O

INTRODUCTION

This book is titled based on what 1 discovered in the books of Matthew 16:18-18 And 1Timothy 3:16 Both scriptures fashioned out how Paul instructs that we may know how we ought to behave ourselves in the house of God, which in the living church of God, the pillar of the ground of the truth. While Jesus in Mathew calls the church as "my Church" I will build my church Both speakers here claim ownership of the church with God which means that we could only function effectively when we begin to see the church as a gift and our being members as a great privilege. The living God has a church which is His house and dwelling place on earth. In our world today, there is much confusion and little understanding of what the church really is. We have names of different kinds of churches and the earnest believer inquires as to which is the right one to belong or be affiliated with. The living church of God is the only right place to where one may go to find the answer. And this word of God is well present in the true church through God's ordained ministers. Having heard this, it is important that we value and attend church fellowship. When you talk about church universally, people think of something stuffy, rigid, judgmental and picky etc.

People often times see the word church as physical structure set up in a particular location, contrary to Christ own view about it. According to R.K. Campbell in his book titled "The Living Church of God", He said that a place of building may be grand European

Cathedral or a simple wooden country church building physically but what our master Jesus literally meant was that the church is a **"called out"** people. Yet the extent to which this sense applies in its general usage 18 very little Politically, the term may be applied to mean an assembly of citizens of a town, but the New Testament teaches that those who follow Christ are called-out people according to 2 Thessalonians 2:13-14. So any reference to as church must be understood to be referring to people and not a building or cathedral. This book highlighted eleven chapters for easier understanding. Apart from the introduction, the

first chapter is bordered on the blood bought. This is to say that the church was purchased with the blood of Jesus and not by material things. Nobody should therefore tamper or joke, or even take for granted what took God the life of His only special son to purchase. If you've been doing so all this while, it will be wise you have a re-think now. The several chapters encourage us to value the importance of the church by seeing it as a precious institution that is owned by God and an avenue of attitudinal change.

Chapter three persuades us to see the need of a regular attendance to church fellowship, irrespective of the distance and fixed times for meetings Chapter four therefore opens our eyes to understanding that it evil and very sinful to distance one's self from church fellowship. Chapter five, teaches us the strength of fellow-shipping together, and the way it strengthens each member, hence we see ourselves as brethren. In chapter six, each worshipper is endowed with the ministry gift and that each of these gifts should be used as a service unto God and to one another.

Chapter seven explains that there is no how a sermon goes out without touching family crises, with its attendant effect in reducing the rate of divorce in the church and in the secular world to the barest minimum; at least some matters will be handled by the priest of that church. Chapter eight went further to tell us more of God's faithfulness and the challenge for us to remain faithful to Him and to one another.

In chapter nine, we discover that the church is like a hospital or workshop, where members both old and new, come for their spiritual and physical needs to be attended to. Chapter ten reveals how God in His word wants us to relate with people of questionable character and the way parents should condition the mind of their children to choose the right footsteps follow and the type of friends to keep. So, all members of the church should know that we are called to serve and sacrifice. Don't wait to be told on what to do for God in the place of your worship. pray that God helps you to understand as you read through. God bless you!

TABLE OF CONTENT

CHAPTER ONE

THE CHURCH AS A 'BLOOD

BOUGHT CONCEPT

The phrase "blood bought 18 very important to both believers (the church) and the pre-believers (the world) alike. It is so because to the church, it will remind them the essence of their faith by bringing them to the full understanding of the sacrifice of our Lord Jesus Christ. And as such reawakens the fainting zeal in their worship and service to God. To the world, it will avail them the privilege to realize that 'somebody' has actually paid the supreme price of reconciling mankind to God. And that there is no need for further works or sacrifice except just to believe in that 'one' who has rescued us from terminal condemnation. No more need for the sacrifice of goats, rams, cows, pigeons, fowls etc, for our cleansing, rather accept the bearer of our burden (JESUS CHRIST) as your Lord and personal Savior.

In order to actualize this purpose, this write-up is divided into four points;

*Definition of the subject matter which will vividly outlay various definitions of blood giving by different schools of thought

* A critical and an in depth discussion of the meaning of blood to different people (religion). The relevance of blood in the medical field (health), as well as in the religious world. Finally, the phrase "purchased by the blood is thoroughly looked at in order to get the true message of the entire article. All these and more are what this topic entails.

According to Oxford Advanced Learner's Dictionary, the word blood is defined as the red liquid that flows through the bodies of humans and animals.

But by Wikipedia world dictionary, blood is seen as a bodily fluid in animals that delivers necessary substances such as nutrient and oxygen to your cells and transport metabolic waste products away from those same cells.

Also by webmd, blood is a constantly circulating fluid providing the body with nutrient, oxygen, and waste removal. It is mostly liquid, with numerous cells and protein suspended in it, making blood "THICKER" than water (pure water).

IMPORTANCE OF BLOOD TO HUMANS

* The average persons (adult) have about five liters (more than a gallon) of blood (www.web MD.com). Humans cannot live without blood. Without blood, the body's organs will not get the oxygen and nutrients they need to survive; we would not keep warm or cold off, fight infections, or get rid of our own waste products. Without enough blood, we will be weakened and die. There are more to this mysterious, life- sustaining fluid called "blood".

MEANING AND IMPORTANCE OF

BLOOD IN SCIENCE/ BIOLOGY/HEALTH "There is life in the

blood"

Biology made us to understand that cells are building blocks of life. And blood is the life wire of body cells; hence the great quote above is not a fallacy. Blood contains proteins, nutrients and oxygen. These contents need to be circulated to all parts of the human body to be supplied with food and oxygen.

If this does not happen, tissues would die and this can cause infections and other problems. Every living parts of the body need oxygen. According to Franklyn Institute,

"the average adult has about five liters of blood living inside of their body coursing through their vessels, delivering essentials elements, and removing harmful waste Without blood the human body would stop working.

* **BLOOD IS THE FLUID OF LIFE:**it transports oxygen from the lungs to the body tissues and carbon dioxide from the body tissue to the lungs.

* BLOOD IS THE FLUID OF GROWTH: it transports nourishment from digestion and hormones from glands throughout the body.
* **BLOOD IS THE FLUID OF HEALTH:** it transport disease fighting substance to the tissues and waste to the kidney. Because blood contains living cells, it is 100% alive.

MEANING OF BLOOD IN CHRISTIANITY

Christianity as a religion regards blood as a supernatural, sacred and sanctimonious substance that should not be wasted or, disregarded. They view it as life and as a powerful sacrificial item which must be respected and not polluted (Lev 17:10 14). For the

Christians, blood is used for sacrifice from the beginning, religious sacrifice is made to include bloodshed. But today, Christians have

Left that to a more spiritual sacrifice. Nevertheless blood still remains a key part in the understanding of sacrifice in Christendom. Christians see Jesus' crucifixion as the "perfect sacrifice" Christ Jesus spilled His blood on the cross for the sins of the world The celebration of Holy Communion is a symbolic celebration of the body and the blood of Christ. So the shedding of Christ's blood, believers now have access to redemption through this act of sacrifice.

THE SACRIFICE OF JESUS A believer accepts Christ's death on the cross to be a necessary atonement for the sins of human kind Apostle Paul wrote "for I deliver to you first of all what I also received, that Christ died for our sins according to the scriptures, and that He was buried and that He rose again on the third day". So, Christ shedding His innocent blood was the final sacrifice which supersedes the need for animal sacrifice. We Christians refer to Jesus' passion as the "ultimate" or "perfect" sacrifice. Christ's death as the ultimate expiration of sins annulled the need for animal sacrifice as done in the Old Testament.

SACRIFICE OF MATYRDOM

This is a major tradition of Christian sacrifice necessary for redemption. We believe that it is only through Christ that we can have redemption these belief and tradition gives the importance of blood in Christian spiritual cleansing. The idea of having sacrifice was bond to the Christian tradition by blood. As we get baptized, we confess that we believe in Jesus, by admitting that Christ's bloodshed on the cross was His self-sacrifice for the forgiveness of our sins. And this proclamation guarantees us redemption. As far as the New Testament is concerned, the sacrificial blood of Christ is expiatory, by the sacrifices of the Old Testament, which were fulfilled and annulled by His greater and more efficacious sacrifice. It was the blood Christ shed, and His death, that provided Christians with redemption for sin.

RELEVANCE OFBLOOD IN CHRISTIANITY

In the Old Testament, for sins to be forgiven, you had to use animals like bulls, and lambs to do some sacrifice. Jesus went to the cross as the Lamb of God with His blood. It cleanses all our sins. His blood is considered holy because He is without any fault and He is the son of God. For us Christians, it is our salvation. Jesus' mercy 1s transparent in the power of the blood. Lev 17:11 says "for the life of a creature is in the blood, and I have

given it to you to make atonement for yourselves on the altar, it the blood that makes atonement for one's life" Blood of the lamb without any defect has to offered for the forgiveness of sins in the old Testament period. In the year of our lord, Jesus is holy and he himself shed his blood for the forgiveness of our sins. Jesus gave His life he ransom for man. In John 3:16, God gave His only son because of His love for us so that we will inherit eternity. So for us, Christians, blood of Jesus is victory over death and evil. The relevance of blood in Christianity is that power of the blood of Jesus Christ. If we recall, in the past (especially old times), different religions had blood sacrifice as a way for their sins to be forgiven. This was also the case for the Jews.

According to the law, almost all things are purified with blood. Heb. 9:22 says "And according to the law almost all things are purified with the blood, and without shedding of blood there is no remission.

There is no remission of sin without the shedding of blood. The blood of animals could not take away sins according to Heb. 10:4 which says "For it is not possible that the blood of bulls and goats could take away sins".

WHY DID MAN NOT PAY FOR HIS SIN WITH HIS OWN

BLOOD?

* Humans cannot give a ransom for his sins Psalm 49:7-9 says "None of them can by any means redeem his brother, nor give to God a ransom for Him". Why? For the redemption of their souls is costly and it shall cease forever that he should continue to live eternally, and not see the pit.

* Humans cannot redeem another from hell but God can give a ransom and redeem humans. Hebrew 13:14 Says "I will ransom them from the power of the grave; I will redeem them from death". Also psalm 49: 15 "But God will redeem my soul from the power of the grave; for he shall receive me' The blood of Jesus can cleanse us and take away our sins. Read 1 John 1:7, Ephesians 1:7, Hebrew 13: 12.

BUT WHY MUST GOD REQUIRE BLOOD FOR

FORGIVENESS?

Life is in the blood. God's righteousness demands payment for sin. In the bible, God made it clear that it is only by the shedding of blood that sins can be forgiven. So the primary purpose of the blood sacrifice is to cover, cleanse, and deliver one from sin and its consequences. The blood of Jesus shed for our sins on the cross paid that price.

PURCHASED BY THE BLOOD (BOUGHT THE BLOOD)

Revelation 5:9 says “they sang new song; you are worthy to take the scroll and break open its seals. For you were killed, and by your sacrificial death you bought for God people from every tribe language, nation, and race Christians today are generally contended in their faith. We become satisfied with what we have been told and the gist of the message we receive and live by it always Jesus has done it all, (Gavin Finley, MD). Sometimes this message looks confusing, this is because to some, conclusion like this may arise: He did it all, there is no need for me to do anything in response. Christ has truly shed His blood. It is in it we had the purchasing price for our salvation. That holy blood of the spotless, sinless sacrificed Lamb of God. The atoning blood of Jesus is the complete and finished sacrifice. It requires nothing else from us Our Lord Jesus who is our bridegroom had fully paid the bridal price of our redemption in His, burial, and resurrection. Christ totally and completely reconciled the account between God and us, His covenant people. The debt for our sin has been cancelled by the shedding of His holy blood. With this shed blood, our Lord Jesus Christ has made total provision for us, His bride (the church).

This is the greatest salvation which the gospel brings. Now the believers must understand and live with this: Jesus purchased the church (believers) with His blood and this makes us important to God. In Acts 20:28, Paul says "Be shepherds of the church of God, which He made His own through the sacrificial death (shedding of blood) of His son. It becomes obvious that we are His (God's) own by the singular reason of the blood- bought which Jesus Christ did for us. God accepted us and designated us His own, what a privilege! Also in Galatians 3:13, Paul also said "but by becoming a curse for us, Christ has redeemed us from the curse that the law brings". For the scripture says "anyone who is hung on a tree 1s under God's curse". Christ did this in order that the blessings which God promised Abraham might be given to the gentiles by means of Christ Jesus, so that through faith we might receive the spirit promised by God. Jesus purchased us with His blood by choosing to die for us on the cross. This is the worst death any one would accept. But just to redeem us back to the Father, He took upon Him the curse we deserved. This is unarguably a supreme sacrifice!

SPIRITUAL SIGNIFICANCE OF BLOOD

“There is life in the blood”

In Lev 17:10-14, we were meant to understand that life is in the blood and that is why we are advised not to eat blood But in the book of Hebrew, we were also made to understand that blood has always been a representative and forerunner to the death of the Messiah, which would result in an everlasting covenant to eternally forgive our sins. God made covenant with Abraham by blood and sacrifice (blood covenant), (Gen 15:9. 10, 17-18). If we remember, Abel's sacrifice was preferred by God to Cain's sacrifice. This was not because the sacrifice of Cain wasn't enough, but because Abel's sacrifice was better, since blood was involved. God forbade the blood of animals from being eaten. This is simply because of what blood represents. It represented the blood and death of Christ. The blood was only to be used for one purpose and that was to atone for our sins. The blood symbolizes cleansing, forgiveness, and life. It was God who created blood with life in it and only the life of one sacrifice would be sufficient to cleanse our sins. So the ultimate sacrifice was that of Jesus, the Lamb of God who takes away the sins of the world- Rev 5:6-9, (John Chingford).

CHAPTER TWO

THE MOST IMPORTANT INSTITUTION

There are so many institutions on this planet earth, but the most important institution that is highly recognized on earth is the "CHURCH". The church is the most important institution on earth, outside of the family. How many Christians regard the local church as of great importance in their life, family, community and world? But in practice, we relegate it to little importance. The church of Jesus Christ is the most important institution in the world. The church, also known as the assemblies of the redeemed, the company of the saints, or the children of God has more significance in the world history than any other group, organization or nation. The church as the most important institution should be seen as the spiritual body of Christ and also a place where people gather to fellowship together, hear the word of God from the preacher, and as Christians have

the opportunity to love and serve one another in accordance with God's command. The church maybe referred to also as the true image, traditionally employed in the bible, to speak of the people of God such as the image of the vineyard, used particularly in the gospel of John. Most people see the church the same way as the government, to be a hierarchy of leaders managing an organization that they engage in but however remain apart from it. For decades now, we've heard the old adage that "the church isn't the building itself, but rather the people inside it. In many people's imaginations, the church remains a bundle of programs, committees, policies, teams, ministers, initiatives, budgets and events. No! Is wisdom to judge things the right and careful way, because they are not always what they seem to be? Remember what the bible says in the epistle of Peter chapter 1 verse 24 and 25 that "all flesh is like grass. And all its glory is like the flower of the grass.

The grass withers, and the flower falls, but the word of the Lord abides forever". The new testament never used the adjectives "catholic "universal" to refer to the church, but does indicate that the local communities are one church, and Christians must always seek to be in concord, and they must extend the gospel of Christ to

the ends of the earth and to all nations, and also know that the church is open to all people and must not be divided.

The gates of Hades, the powers of death, etc, will prevail against every institution but one, the church. Jesus said to Simon Peter in the gospel of Matthew 16:18that "you are Peter, and on this rock (Peter), I will build my church, and the gates of hell shall not prevail against it', and He meant it. This assures us that the church is a community instituted by Christ Himself. God sanctioned the church to care of His people and advance His interests in the world. Therefore the church should be seen as the pillar and foundation of the truth!

CHAPTER THREE

CHURCH ATTENDANCE I

Church attendance is very important because the bible tells us the need to go to church, so that we can worship God with other believers and be taught His word for our spiritual growth, (Acts 2:42, Heb 10-25).

The church is a place where believers can LOVE another (1 John 4:12), ENCOURAGE one another (Heb 3:13), EXHORT one another, it say's "and let us consider one another to provoke unto love and to good works."(Heb 10:24), SERVE one another, it say's "for brethren ye have been called unto liberty; only use not liberty for an occasion to the flesh, but by love serve one another". (Gal 5:13), INSTRUCT one another (Rom 15:14), HONOUR one another (Rom 12:10) and be KIND and COMPASSIONATE to on another (EPH 4:32). When a person trusts Jesus Christ for salvation, he or she is made a member the body of Christ (1 COR 12:27). For a church body to function properly, all of its "body parts" need to be present (1 Cor 12:14-20)

A believer will never reach full spiritual maturity without the assistance and encouragement of other believers (1 Cor. 12:21-26) Church attendance, participation, and fellowship should be a regular aspect of a believer's life Weekly church attendance is not what a believer should wait to be reminded of regularly, but someone who truly belongs to Christ should have a desire to worship God, receive his word and fellowship with other believers. Jesus didn't die for religious system or for a particular nation. For the scripture says "how God anointed Jesus of Nazareth with the holy ghost and with power, who went about doing good, and healing all that were oppressed by the devil for God was with him" (Acts 10:38).He shed His blood to purchase the church, meaning that the church is the most important thing Christ is concerned about.

Parents need the church because that is where their children's conducts and concepts are molded. If we create the impression that the congregation, which is the church is not important, we lose our children; but when we instill the actual meaning and the importance of the local church in their minds, they will grow along side with the teaching and mould their lives around it. (Mathew 19:13 says then were there brought unto him little children, that he should put his hands on them and pray and the disciples rebuked them. (Gen 18:10,1 Tim 3:4)

TEN GOOD REASONS TOATTEND CHURCH SERVICES

1. **TO HAVE FELLOWSHP WITH THE CRUCIFIED AND RISEN CHRIST:** if you knew that Jesus himself was going to be at a particular place on a regular basis, would you not be motivated to go? The local Christian congregation is the place where Christians gather publicly to commune with their risen Savior. When they worship, the Lord Himself is present and He promised to be where ever Christians gather. "For where two or three come together in my name there am I with them" (Matt 18:20) and "surely I am with

you always, to the very end of the age (Matt 28:20)

2. **TO BE FORGIVEN:** why come to church? Because the Lord Jesus is there. And He is there primarily to give forgiveness to all who repent and believe. Proclaiming the full forgiveness that Jesus won for us on the cross is the main point of all Christian worship services. These are the amazing things about our God. He comes among His people not primarily to receive but to give the precious forgiveness of sins.

3. **TO HEAR THE VOICE OF GOD:** Never before have people been confronted with so many voices. Never before have people been confronted with so many choices. All the more reasons to go to0 church regularly. For there the voice of God Himself speaks to us through sermon, scripture liturgy and hymnody. God speaks to His people as a whole and He speaks to them individually, guiding them into truth, reminding them of what is right, warning them about what is wrong. His voice is a voice of strength and comfort, a voice of sanity among the insanity. His is the voice that tells the truth when so many other voices cannot be trusted.

4. **GROW IN THE KNOWLEDGE OF THE BIBLE, GOD'S WORD:**Here you areresponding to a common excuse. "I don't need to goto church to hear the word; I can read the bible onmy own On the other hand, private study of God'sword is wonderful, but private study of the scripture must not be a substitute for hearing the preacher's word. There are two reasons; the first is theological, and the second is practical. Because the pastor, who holds the divinely appointed preachingoffice is by God's will the chief teacher of God'sword, the one through whom Christ Himself speaks(it says" he that heareth you, heareth me and he that despiseth you,

despiseth me also, Luke 101 2Tim 4:1-5, Eph. 4:11-16, 11im 4:18-16, Heb 13.17 The pastor has been blessed with the gift teaching Furthermore, he has gone through extensive tutelage and study so as to become "specialist" in handling God's word.

5. TO FEED THE SOUL: Feed the soul? Does the soul need nourishment? According to the scripture, yes! There we are reminded that "man does not live on bread alone but on every word that comes from the mouth of the Lord" (Deut. 8:3, Matt 4:4). There we are encouraged. "Like newborn babies, long for the pure milk of the word so that by it you may grow in respect to salvation" (1 Peter 2:2). God's word is the best food for the soul. Public worship is the best place to give your soul the word of God which is the nourishment it needs In another place Jesus says, "do not work for the food which perishes, but for the food which endures to eternal life, which the son of man will give to you (1 John 6:37). How tragic to see people zealously provide for their bodies but leave their souls so famished?

6. TOBE LOVED AND ENCOURAGED: Why does one have to go to church regularly? To feel the affection amongst the brethren and also get some motivations both spiritually and physically. We all have troubles. We all face dilemmas and disappointments. We all wrestle with discouragement and heartache. What God said to Adam applies to us all: it is not good for man to be alone" Coming to church means interacting with your fellow Christians, the body of Christ. It means receiving an encouraging word. It means having someone listen to the preacher's word which is the word of God. More profoundly, it is often through His body, the church that Christ speaks the comfort and crucial direction that we need. How often one Christian will have a spiritual insight that benefits another. Come to church to be loved and be encouraged.

7. TO BE PRAYED FOR: Jesus once promised "If two of you agree on earth about anything that they may ask, it shall be done for them by my Father who is in heaven" (Matt 18:19). There is power when the people of God pray. But for those unfortunate souls who have cut themselves off from regular attendance at the Christian assembly, their needs are unknown, and they pray alone. An often overlooked reason to come to church is to be prayed for.

8. TO LOVE AND ENCOURAGE YOUR FELLOW CHRISTIAN: At the heart of theChristian ethics is the obligation to love ourneighbors as ourselves. Jesus sharpens this in thegospel of John 13:34-35 where He says, a new commandment I give to you that you love oneanother, even as I have loved you, that you also loveone another. By this all men will know that you aremy disciples if you have love for one another Theapostle Paul echoes this when he writes in one of hisepistles that we, "bear one another's burdens, and thereby fulfill the law of Christ (Gal 6:2) and “sothen while we have opportunity, let us do good to allpeople and especially to those who are of thehousehold of the faith" (Gal 6:10). Failing to attend public worship regularly not only transgresses thethird commandment ('remember the Sabbath day tokeep it holy'); it also transgresses the law of Christ, tolove one's fellow Christians and to bear theirloveburdens. When we refuse to gather with our fellowChristians, then this is not love! By such refusal welose touch with them and in most cases have no ideawhat they are going through. How can weencourage and help them then? Furthermore, ourabsence in church services is a powerful non-verbaldiscouragement to them. While our presence is apowerful non-verbal encouragement, to other fellowChristians.

9. TO WORSHIP: That Christians are to worship God publicly is a biblical given. Behind this given is the reality that we are creatures and God is the creator. Everything we are and have 1s a gift from Him. Therefore God richly deserves our worship, our praise, thanks and prayers. Because God through Christ has forgiven us and given us eternal life out of pure grace. He richly deserves our public praise and thanks through words and songs.

10. TO PROMOTE THE GOSPEL: Remember, the Christian church exists in order to "make disciples of all nations" (Matt 28:19). We exist to tell the good news that through Christ's crucifixion and resurrection, God has forgiven humanity and offers heaven as a gift to those who believe this. The church's main mission is to populate heaven and depopulate hell.

All these and more are seen and achieved in the most important institution which is the church no other institution can give out what God institution can give. So regard and respects the assembly of the saints.

CHAPTER FOUR

CHURCH ATTENDANCE II

Attending believers' church services together is a vital part of God's plan for us. However the poor attendance of some church service shows that many do not understand this important teaching of the New Testament. Most Bible believing churches Schedule at least three services a week; however fewer members attend service regularly. Church attendance is the subject of a "tongue in the cheek according to Cooper Abrahams (), Romans 12:1 2, and I Cor. 16:13. Those that attend Sunday morning services love the preaching, those that attends Sunday night service love the church those that attends midweek service love the Lord. Oftentimes, we hear references to some in the church today as "fair weather Christians. These are the ones who would miss church service because of rain and

other non-important 1s8ues God says in Heb. 10:19-25 "not forsaking the assemblies of the brethren together.

Here He teaches us several things to do as regards to church attendance. The church is very important in our lives. It will make your children or those under you to care to ask, are we not going to Sunday school fellowship today? Rather than asking for something else. This happens because you have made church service attendance very important in the lives of your family members, as stated by Jim and Carolyn Murphy. What about you who stay in business, watch TV, play games and other pleasures while time is up for church service? You are telling your neighbors that your church pastor's belief doesn't matter. If not, tell me what Jesus died or shed His blood for? We should attend church services and be willing to involve ourselves in the activities in the church because it is the most important thing to Jesus our Lord (Luke 10:42, Ps 27:4). As a true believer in Christ, church attendance should not be a suggestion, rather should be a command (Lev 19:1-17, Exodus 14:1; 20:111). The bible is not a book filled with suggestions, it is the word of God and it commands that we attend our local assembly and not when we have less chance, no matter the distance and the

time fixed (Heb 10:28-26) It is sinful to abstain from church services without a grave cause you not miss church service when you have a problem church service regular attendance 18 a matter of commitment and it's really necessary (Luke 9:62 Acts 442); It was the problem that Sister Martha had with Jesus whereas Sister Mary was appreciated due to her sticking around Jesus whenever He visits their house. You are therefore encouraged to form a habit of attending church services regularly. The presence of God is never boring, you're been refreshed, your faith and commitment encourages the weak ones. Throughout the old and new testament, the necessity of setting aside some days in a week to be at God's presence was never overruled. If the son of God felt the need to attend a house of worship regularly, we as followers of His should do no less. The Sabbath, an Old Testament tradition gives way in the New Testament for gathering to worship on the first day of the week as a commemoration of Jesus' resurrection. The day is not essential rather, the gathering together is. Reasons are that relationships are an important part of human life. We are not created to live in isolation according to the book of Luke 4:16. However it is obviously encouraged to attend church services regularly because it is God's command for us to be faithful to it. One should be very careful to take the things of the church lightly, if one really understood the actual meaning of the church in biblical context. The way one attends church services can be seen as a barometer of one's dedication and commitment to the Lord. It can also show a lack of inward peace and interest to show fellowship with the Lord. So, not attending church services regularly shows lack of concern for others. It is a selfish and an inconsiderate act to do as a Christian. A church member does not show love and concern for others when he avoids their company. The way we change our mind to attend church fellowship can inspire others to do same.

CHAPTER FIVE:

VERY SINFUL

As Christians filled with the Holy Spirit, we only recognized sin mainly as sexual misconduct. Fighting, stealing, adultery and fetish practices, while the unintentional ones are not inclusive.

That is, you can go ahead to indulge in them, it doesn't matter. No! (James 4:13-17, Luke 12:42)

When a Christian forgets that he should be faithful and anticipates the manifestation of his Lord but instead romances with laziness as the order of the day, he is therefore indeed very sinful. It is a sin to stay out of the church service when you know you should be there. It is a grievous sin for a person under the profession of any status to be carefree to what Jesus died for. A young man was arrested and brought to a police cell. Suspects who were there before him questioned him on the crime that caused his arrest. After the explanations, the inmates later frowned at him that he should have

Committed a bigger crime that would justify his suffering. So they coached him on how to commit heavy crimes. Have you noticed that people only die for what benefits them more? But in this case, Jesus Christ may not be playing a fool as a person would conclude from a distance. He died innocently for a crime that does not concern Him. He actually died to save us. What an irreparable love in other to save His enemies according to the gospel in John 1:11-12 He shed His blood after He was nabbed by His kidnappers. His blood was shed for the church. Importantly, if we are reasonable enough, concerted effort should be directed towards upholding the church that He died for with all potentials within our reach. This challenge include coming together to worship, honor and to show respect to God. You already know that sin is sin everywhere. True children of God should fear sin. Reason is that every sin committed will cause the victim more harm than what he thinks is there to benefit. The worst is that sin whether small or great separates one from the presence of God. It didn't go down well with Adam's household. What about the nation Israel, anytime they misbehave, God hands them over to their enemies. Sit up and be more conscious of sin. It makes the offenders smell like a he- goat. It is somehow fairer to be seen as a commissioned sinner

than as a hypocrite. By being born again, it confirms a serious oath to aide in of the Lord all the days of your life Being at large in Christ amounts to insubordination to the body of Christ, it is not only the ministers of God that bears the burden of the church, it is mandated on every believer. You as a human being were made by God to live in the atmosphere of worship. Therefore man is a worshipper by creation and when he is not directed to the right God, he chooses to worship anything that resembles a creator to him. Public Worship is essential than private ones at home or in the office. In the Old Testament, God told Moses to take His people out for worship at a designated place which pharaoh objected. Through the power of technology, people everywhere are tempted to stay at home to worship. With the sophistication of electronic gadgets in every nooks and cranny, the interest to worship via radio, TV, internet, or even in our cars instead of converging together in the church are not farfetched. It will just take the grace and power of the Holy Spirit to overcome such influence.

They may look real but not reasonable. The level of the Hi-tech attraction should not deny us the real interaction with other saints when we sit together When we come to the house of God, we come to show love and appreciation to God first, then to one another as brethren. David in the Psalms said “I will testify and

pay my vows before the congregation of God's people”. The same word of God affirms that when we come together, the blood of Jesus cleanses us from all unrighteousness When you meet people of the same faith, needs are identified and attended to. If you had stayed at home and worshipped, you wouldn't have figured out some people to attend to or the opportunity of being attended to, or even realizing that God can use you to assist others come out of their challenges. When you don't know that you are a blessing, you will not be useful in God's house because one may not benefit from your values. We should not just be there' in God's house or offer 'out of the lips' services to God according to apostle Peter in 1 Peter 2:9. We are kindred in Christ and fellow citizens. This is a nomenclature out there in the societal system. More at home, Christian people should have in depth knowledge of where we belong. Our privilege in Christ right now has made us to be members of Jesus' clan, whether spiritual or physical. Like today, jobs, care, attention, etc are being offered based on one’s locality or relationship and not even necessarily by merit. This is the extent of the degeneration of our societal values and morality. If you know that you are of the same kindred and fellow citizen in Jesus Christ, then it will give you a ground to

even assume that your challenges are already being taken care of before you present your demand. Good reason for this assumption is that Jesus Christ your senior brother had passed through all these “ups-and-downs” and yet emerged victorious.

CHAPTER SIX

STRENGTH OF FELLOWSHIP

The belief that unity is power is still reasonable enough. You can break a stick of a single broom but you can't break a bundle of broom sticks, this is also agreeable. When two or more persons urinate on one spot at the same time, it produces more foam, according to an Igbo adage. The same applies to literal philosophy that the church is God's great asset to humanity that is why anywhere the church is sited, its span is beyond limit. According to 1Cor 12:26 and 1Cor 1:9, the awareness of the strength that is in fellowship comes true when we come together. It is by the time we come together irrespective of our pedigree that we become sensitive to one another and hence enables us to discover our values. It is by the time we discover our values that we do away with the idea of casual attendance to church, whereby we disturb God with bundles of needs and challenges without knowing what we should do for God

as an individual or as group. According to the book of Hebrews chapter 1 vs. 29, nothing does itself. Even in our homes we should realize that God created us to go ahead subduing, replenishing and developing our grounds. God can't build a worshiping place for you God won't give you power (electricity) to run the church. God won't give pews, or decorate your church environment for you. God won't buy you musical instrument, God won't buy furniture or church vehicles for you, rather you and I should be responsible for the growth of the church of God. No wonder Jesus called His disciples gods. In other words, when you realize that you are a god, you can now occupy as today's oracle. No wonder some casual believers do wait to be told what to do even when they are members of that particular church. They are good in waiting for announcement, appointment, invitation and levying. Even when they are been levied, they do argue that everybody should pay equal amount without considering that all fingers are not equal. Do you know why God pulled you out from where you were into that church? Consequently the church has been static and undermined because of your ingenuity. Smart ones like you even dodge responsibilities, even when announced that such event

will take place at a particular date. We need to live close to the church as far as familiarity, attendance and nearness are concerned If opportunity calls that you are living close to the church, it will help you to pick other duties. If a person has needs, you can be the first person to help out. When one suffers, every member should feel it (Rom 13:7.14, Heb. 10:34). Do you know that your neighbors will simply join your local church when they observe your cares to one another? This was seriously practiced by the apostles of old, they were all engaged selling out their properties, sharing the profits to help those that have pressing needs. No wonder the scripture enjoins that the earnest expectations are waiting for the manifestation of the people of God which is the church". Though God will supply all our need as affirmed by Paul in Philippians 4:19, He will only do this when we have complied because he must meet needs through human beings. As a spirit filled child of God, make yourself to be felt by the church, by making your due contributions and also attending to your fellow brothers needs and challenges.

CHAPTER SEVEN

NECESSITY OF THE MINISTRY

Without ministry, we are just bodiless, therefore ministry is a sacrificial service. You see that coming into the body of Christ makes you a child and no good child claims to know better than his father. From time to time God calls us His little children. Do you still see yourself as God's child or otherwise. When you do, then you will understand that you are to serve with humility and faithfulness (Isaiah2:3, Micah 4:1, Gen. 49:1, Jer. 50:5). Attending regularly to church services, no matter the session will help you to know what God wants you to know and do. 1 strongly believe that God knows you; I mean the entirety of you. Does this make any sense to you? God, Himself even called Samuel by his name; though he did not understand, if not for Eli that put him through. God also gave Abraham a call by his name and he responded because of his openness of heart. God also called Saul before sending him to fulfill a divine mandate. There are many things He would want you to

know. But you will not know them in a day neither will you in a single service attendance. It is when you come close to someone that you can smell the odour of his mouth. Of course you cannot claim to know someone without staying with the person for a good number of times. My dear, always be inquisitive to know what God has for you each time you fellowship in His presence.

Remember that Isaac was inquisitive to know from his father Abraham the situation on ground; hence he asked "I have seen the fire wood, water jar, what of the animal for the sacrifice? I am surprised that many church members have just made church service attendance lackadaisical; they forget to get their mindset ready for God and simply arrive there without a desire at heart. Forgetting that going to church service without a burning desire may amount to disaster. God said in the scripture "ask me concerning the works of my hand", He also said "ask and it shall be given unto you". No wonder Jesus asked the blind Batimaeus, "What do you want me to do for you'"? Similarly, Peter asked the physically challenged man at the Beautiful gate "rise up and walk" after he complained that "I have no man". I suppose you are like one of these men.

I therefore put it to you to always develop thirst for expectations each time you want to go to God's presence. When you do not know what expect, you can direct your attention to the theme that service. This may be a guide to getting you expectations met. According to Ephesians 4:11, 2Timothy 16-17, you can get it right on time that God work through ministries by the Holy Spirit, Each minister with a unique ministerial gift operates differently from the other to the edifying of the children of God Nevertheless, no any ministry should be overruled or neglected Child of God can a good parent feed invisible children? No! Parents can only feed their children when they are physically available. Your pastor, the head of the local church can only feed you when you attend church services. If you can't come to church service, the pastor will not carry the message of that day to your house, neither will the church carry that day's music to your house. This in essence means that you should blame yourself for missing out in God's presence each day you are absent. It also robs you of the commitment that God and your brethren expect from you. This directly or indirectly affects the faith of others and in general the unity and strength of the body of Christ

CHAPTER EIGHT

MARRIAGE STABILITY

Marriage as an institution has been facing enormous challenges ever. This is the only institution that 1s meant to last without dissolution unless death separates the union. Today, the rate of divorce is too high due to lack of proper marital management. Satan knows that it is the only institution that God says that he who engages in it will find favor. So God established and reorganized marriage as a divine institution. The couples involved are meant to be a helpmate for each other (Gen 2:18-24). We should understand that marriage was introduced for the purpose of founding and maintaining a family. Marriage is not meant for babies but for the grown-ups, who can fend for themselves. Therefore the desire to marry is normal, legitimate and proper. Both parties who wish to marry should consider what will be the character and influence of the home they are about

to make. However in order to minimize the high rate of marriage abuse, it is therefore necessary that issues on marriage should be included I seminars, workshops, church services, etc. So attending church services and fellowship offers marriage stability to intending ones and married ones as well. Family issues are thought in the fellowship and church services. Let me tell you a little story, a couple in a certain church had a face. off on the

Saturday before Sunday which they couldn't cope up with. As God may have it, on getting to church out of their usual way the minister of God didn't know that he resolved that issue during ministration, they came back from fellowship and regretted what they did without a resolution before going to service. Be that as it may, one of the pastor's burdens as a contribution to their flock is to ensure that either through prayers or admonitions that the couples under his care do enjoy their marriages instead of enduring it. We should bear in mind that when a family is in shamble, it affects the church. And when the church is affected, the pastor may be affected also. Moreover, welfare of the members of the church should be the key interest of the pastor. If a shepherd feeds the sheep very well, he will have enough milk.

When the pastor of the church is not concerned about the well-being of the congregation that church may not be able to respond to his personal challenges. Nevertheless. There will be no record of meaningful development in terms of numerical explosions and infrastructural achievements in the church. The church as an institution, apart from court wedding, is the first body empowered to conduct a marriage union. More so, the church should be on the front line to help reduce the high rate of divorce in our society. They can achieve this by using the biblical standards to sensitize the couples and the intending ones (Col 3:1-8). Other ways of achieving this desire is by one-on-one counseling, where marital experiences that concern others could be used as a deterrent and as an emphasis to enhance understanding of the subject matter. Being a revered man (pastor), he is duty bound to keep either of the party to avoid further damage until the tension is controlled. A constant teaching that mentions marital issues equally makes spouses too be conscious of them as it concerns their marriage. Actually, your local churches do assist in your marriage growth according to 1Peter3:1-7. Here Peter explains marriage relationships which borders on the role of each party involved in the

marriage In addition, parents should as we involve their children in fellowship and church activities where they would learn some principles and guidelines that may assist them in choosing the right partner for marriage: This reduces the chances of making wrong choices and prevent divorce (Rom 23:13)

God Is Faithful

Faithfulness is one of the attributes of God. It is also one of the important virtues of a leader. Our misconduct can't make God to be unfaithful in His ways. He likes to entrust great grace on faithful servants. Therefore being faithful is an act of holding on, abiding to instruction that is given by your superior. God will always do what He says He will do and He invites us into partnership with His son. The book of 1 Cor1:9 tells us that God is faithful who has called us into fellowship of His son I have good news for you! This good news is that God is faithful to keep His promises to us and forevermore. However when we say God is faithful we mean that we can trust Him, rely on Him, depend on Him totally and without reservation. He is faithful to protect you from temptation and evil. Thank God for the church. The church is a gift to you. It's a gift in the sense that when

you engage yourself with a true church, you will embrace man opportunities for your deliverance, healing and reconciliation for righteous living. For encouragement and for motivation8. The church the only institution that Jesus Christ is the Head, of course you know whatever Jesus Christ hate must be seriously bad. Inside the church abound prayers, teachings, dancing, testimonies, etc. The type of entertainments that go on in the church is enough to turn off your worries. Do you know that having been in the church for many years, you must have been acquainted with the affairs and the tenets of the church, which makes you love everything about God and the body of Christ in its totality? You never lose anything staying in the presence of God. Not at all!

Analysis Of God's Faithfulness

Dr. M. Dewane Anderson in his book "growing in the knowledge of the lord" posited that our society has been programmed to question everything. Most of us have fallen into that same pattern of thinking. In this day, we really need to know if we can trust God. According to Apostle Paul in 1 Cor. 1:9, we base our trust in the accumulation of the evidences of the things we have personally witnessed and experienced history

demonstrates the faithfulness of God. The bible tells us that He is faithful. This therefore establishes basis of our firm faith. 1Cor 10:13 ensures further confirmation of the faithfulness of God. God accordingly in Deuteronomy 32:4 (GNT) does what is right and fair in relation to being faithful to our prayers. God's word is reliable, God's promises are sure, and God's power is unchangeable. This means that when you pray, you can stand on what God has said. When you are challenged and feel weak, you can rely on God's promises. He is really able to save completely. All His messages and words are true, that when you come through Jesus Christ, the answer to your needs and challenges is on the way (2 Tim 1:12, NKJV). When we consider the protection that God gives, and commit anything to Him, He is faithful to keep it. No device of the enemy shall ever prosper against you. And no vile and destructive scheme will ever succeed. By the way, haven't you notice God's forgiveness to all who come to Him? His grace, which I am a living proof of, is so amazing. Throughout time, we see His faithful forgiveness. For example, people commit a lot of outrageous wicked and vile sins, yet when they turn to the Lord and confess their sis, God faithfully forgives them. Consider David, who hosted another man's wife and committed

fornication, lies, and plotted murder condemning Uriah, the husband of the woman to death to cover his sin, and pretended to be just and right. But in all his actions, God sent Nathan the prophet to David to let him know that He saw all he did. But immediately he was convicted of his sin, he confessed them and repented of the sins he committed, and God forgave him. Indeed my readers, I want you to know that God's faithfulness is not comparable. It is therefore a challenge that we should be faithful to God, our partners, congregation and employers. Nevertheless, God is God, and He is faithful! God is faithful to save keep, protect and forgive us in everything (Ps. 108:4)

CHAPTER TEN

ENJOYING THE CHURCH VICTORY

Understanding the basics of the church will dare you to appreciate the fact that power invested in the church by God is more than the power that Nigeria constitution gives to the law enforcement agents Jesus Christ has dashed us complete Victory over the devil and his cohorts. Indeed, that was His parts. Our part is to enforce and sustain the victory, then, live our lives as members of the purchased church. All this while, we have seen how vital it is that we know whom we are in Christ Jesus. When we received the lord Jesus Christ into our hearts, we were born into the beloved family of God. Then, our names were written in the divine archive of heaven. Nevertheless, we have a divine authority which we may exercise to control the enemy's scheme here on earth. This is an exciting experience we will continue to enjoy.

You Are Named In Heaven And Elsewhere

The story told in Luke chapter 10 on account of the 70 disciples whom Jesus sent out to preach the gospel of the kingdom. You can see how excited they were as they returned, adding that demons obeyed them as they spoke in the name of Jesus. Surprisingly, the Lord shocked them by telling them an unusual word "notwithstanding in this rejoice not, that the spirit are subject unto you; but rather rejoice, because your names are written in heaven. (Luke 10:200). Actually their source of power was not merely mentioning Jesus' name, rather it all happened in their relationship with Him. We cannot afford to put faith in a "magical formular" of marathon words. It takes more than right words to face and combat the devil; it simply takes a right relationship with Almighty God the father. When we confess Jesus as our Lord and Savior, our names are recorded in the network of heaven. You receive authority according to John 1:12 "but as many as received him, to them gave the power to become the sons of God, even to them that believed on his name. This belongs to special sons and daughters of God. Also note that this relationship with Christ is the source of our authority over the enemy.

Acknowledge the fact that the first son of Queen Elizabeth of England has a great deal of influence and au

thority in the kingdom of Great Britain When the Queen sends him to represent her, his relationship with her would cause this son's words to carry great authority, not just that he said I come in the name of Queen Elizabeth but his authority would be as a result of his relationship with the Queen, his mother. Not just the word he said. If I stood in the Nigerian National senate and said "I speak to you all in the name of President Mohammed Buhari, I would be laughed to scorn. Why? Because I have no right to speak in his name since we are not related at all. For these corresponding reasons, our words addressed to the devil have power only if we are rightly related to Jesus who triumphed over all the principalities and powers of the devil. Even the demons know your stand with Jesus now irrespective of the church you belong. There is a funny story in acts of Apostles which continues and supports this concept. Apostles Paul had great breakthrough in releasing people from demonic powers. A Jewish man by name of sceva had seven sons they took it upon themselves to try Paul's "method" of casting out demons using the name of the lord Jesus. Coming across a demon

man, they addressed in the name of Jesus, who possessed Saul preaches, I command you to come out The evil spirit replies "I know Jesus and Paul, but who are you. The demon was angry at this false claim to Jesus Name because these boys had no relationship with Jesus. The demon then empowered the lunatic with great strength. He attacked them severely and drove them out of the Scene naked. Acts 19:13-16. They used right words but didn't have a right relationship with God. Their names weren't written in heaven. It is interesting to know that both Jesus' name and that of Paul were known by the demons. What of your own name though you have been too long in the church? Demons do check this record of names before they respond to your charge. They know well who is there and who is not there. If your name is there, you have power to resist and make him flee any scene. You are part of Gods eternal purpose and have been given the power to evangelize this earth.

CHILDLIKE FATH:- Key to kingdom authority, Luke 10:21 says "in that hour Jesus rejoiced in spirit, and said, I thank thee O father, Lord of heaven and earth, that thou hast hid these things from the wise and prudent, and hast revealed them unto babes; even so, father for so it seemed good in thy sight. Jesus also said in Mark 10:15 that "verily I say unto you, whosoever shall not receive the kingdom of God as a little child, he shall not enter therein In other words, the key to kingdom power and authority is simple childlike faith as children of the king. Because we are related to great, we are also great. God delights to use his children to defeat the enemy. He did this by choosing a young shepherd boy to slay the great giant, Goliath (1 Sam. 16:1-13). God can use any of his children like you out there. If you know who you are in Christ and act in the authority of His name as a church, indeed, our heavenly father finds great joy and delight in seeing His sons and daughters put the devil in his place.

CHAPTER ELEVEN

PLACE OF NEEDS MET

Whether we consider it real or not, life is more realistic in the spiritual realm than in the physical. The spiritual realm controls the physical, to live successfully, it belivs us to do some rapid investment more in the spirit realm. The investments are done through prayers and word force. King David the very man that is after God's own heart opined that "the zeal of the house of the Lord has eaten him up". He also added that he is always happy when they say let us go to the house of God (the church). Do you think that this applies to you If not, you cannot be a useful tool in the hands of God as you will lack the driving zeal to work for Him. That zeal is your propelling force. It moves you and holds you on for performance. According to the book of the Acts of the Apostles chapter 3, if the incapacitated man at the gate called

Beautiful did not imbibe that the church is the place of solution, nothing on earth would have directed his attention towards that place and of course his high expectation was guaranteed through the dynamic presence of Peter and John Where do you look to for a solution? If people then look on you, can you generate anything to help their condition instead of compounding their case from bad to worse? Recall that the children of Israel were bitten by serpent due to their unfaithfulness. But solution through the intervention of God came by demanding on them to prepare and set up a statue and gain freedom by focusing their attention on the object. Of course, not all were willing to comply, but to those who were sensitive testified of God's overwhelming deliverance. Your simple obedience will give you in into God's provision and allocation.

PLACE AND CONTRIBUTION

Child of God, don't become too independent as a general overseer, or too gifted, talented, familiar, or popular to the extent that you see no importance of your PLACE and CONTRIBUTION in the church of God. Reason is that we are in the Last days. Christianity is in the injury time now. Just like in the game of football, at the 18 meters yard box, where the opponent, as an attacker is struggling to overcome both the active

defenders and the goalkeeper in order to score a goal. At this point every defending player has to be on the alert in other to frustrate the mission of his opponent. Every core Christian occupies a place in the church no matter where you are coming from. The enemies of the faith will be interested to make you feel irrelevant to the assembly. Moreover, your place is your position. Your position well defined determines your activities. In Hosea 6:1, God said woe to any person who is idle in His house". Idleness in the church confirms you are an 1dol. And an idol if not controlled on time may lead you into idolatry. Not defining your place in the church will make you irresponsible. Understand your placement in the church and then become a contributor. Your contribution indicates your identification. In this case you will not wait to be told what to do and when to do it. Render your financial contribution by offerings and tithe paying. Render other services that you are naturally skilled for in the church, because the church needs it. God needs you as well as the society, avoid being brother/ sister nobody Understand this simple truth. The church is a place where needs are met. This is pretty true because people will leave their houses to church

service very battered, offended, hungry, sick unattended to, hopeless, contused, disappointed humiliated, denied, misunderstood, abused thirsty and heartbroken. But the assurance is that they go home rehabilitated and polished after their encounter with the presence of God. The church is a hospital, workshop, bar, school, training ground, relaxation, and recreation center for all. So don't increase the sorrow of people coming to the church.

The pastor and other trained workers should through the help of the Holy Spirit assist them to be welcomed. Desist from making the church appear hostile to people by the way you treat them. Mind you; any hungry soul you refused to treat well will be accounted for on the last day. So don't push them up and down with your 'extra- righteousness and old membership syndrome. God knew this and according to the book of Ephesians 4:1-5, overloaded the church with the gifted men and women. This gift and the gifted should display it in wisdom and understanding. A teacher was teaching somewhere and eventually, asked a question. What is fellowship? A little boy answered "when two fellows are in one ship"! Where then is your own ship (Church)? What ship are you in? Do you feel any need to have fellowship with the saints of God? All about you is important to God and to His church, including all that

you are and all you have whether inside and outside the church. lt is even a shame that the pastor of your local church doesn't Know you personally, which may be as a result of hiding your identity and potential. May be you are the type that comes late to fellowships and leaves earlier before the benediction is said due to your numerous secular engagements. And sometimes, you don't even attend at all. How long will you remain like this? Have you not been told that your attitude in the church has changed your name and identity into something funny? You can ask some serious members and neighbors, they will definitely tell you what they call you nowadays. Behold, no matter how clever you think you are in avoiding responsibilities in the church and to your pastor, one day as a human being, you must need your church's attention and assistance either in funeral or celebration matters. Actually, the church can meet your need but you must do your individual part. Start contributing meaningfully to the upkeep and all round development of that church: this is the only reason why God placed you there. If for no other reason, the church can be a blessing to you through concerted prayers.

GOOD COMPANY God said it very plain that His church must match on and nothing on earth can stop it! The above statement simply highlights God's stand point and involvement. It does not exonerate us from making our own individual contributions. We are in a society that is characterized with corruption. Just like fishes in the river that cannot deny water, so nobody should claim innocent of it. Gods willing, there are still some people in the land who refused to soil their hands with the prevailing trend of corruption. During the time of the three (3) Hebrew boys, they actually chose to die rather than to compromise on eating the king's food that is defiling Moses had similar opportunity to enjoy in the kings palace, but he sacrificed it. He chose to suffer with his brethren than to enjoy the pleasures of Egypt. Yes, Christianity is not by gain saying, what is on demand now is doing and living it for people to see. Anything you sacrificed because of the gospel is your own price tag. Christianity costs Jesus Christ. Therefore it will equally cost you and I. What it costs you is your defense. It is like a lady who married as a virgin. You find out that often, she will be proud to say that she never defiled herself before marriage. As a believer in Christ, you are faced daily with things that could put you off if you are not focused. Godliness is transparent, selfless, and

replete in integrity excellent character. The godly person views personal relationship as one of life's highest priorities and failure in these areas as most serious. Therefore parents apart from being careful on how to relate with people around them, should also help their children to have a good company since it is understandable that evil communication corrupts good manner (1 Cor. 15:33). As we know that you must form a company with others, one should at least look for good ones. Friends are important to people but we must start early to help them join good spirited mate. Be it age mate, classmate, business mate, etc. Paul the apostle quotes from a third century BC Athenian writer, Menander, to show that our lives are influenced by what we believe and whom we associate with. We should befriend right ones and not to join gangsters. Of course it is true that friendship with the world is an enmity with God. According to a native adage, which says "that when a good goat moves with a bad one, it starts behaving exactly like the bad ones? In Proverbs 27:28, Solomon xrayed what happens when an interest is gradually developed on evil. The consequence is that the evil will destroy you without apology because what a man desires is what he sees. Our wards need a close

attention in other to then to the right peer group You should endeavor provide a wholesome atmosphere has is the reasons why your children which are important to you should be closer to God and attend fellowship on regular bass. Don't say that they are too young and yet to learn anything, it is not true! As a panacea for go0d leaving, convey them from school. Workshop, and market place to fellowship or church service according to the days of weekly church programs. Correspondingly, our adult member should do likewise from anywhere he/she is and retire at fellowship venue, Desist from always ending your day where canopies and chairs are arranged for eating, drinking, watching films or perhaps at funeral/ wedding ceremony etc Otherwise, you may lose your identity as a Christian. Again weekly services are very important and helpful. It will keep you in the right track if strictly adhered to.

CHAPTER TWELVE

WHAT ATTRACTS LIFE AND DEATH

TO A CHURCH?

Honestly, we have in one way or the other seen ourselves or have presided over a church that seem to be alive and powerful including another that spiritually inactive. Jim and Carolyn Murphy shaved a pathetic story that was said by Dr Kenneth Hagin in his international Ministers Manual.

Accordingly, it was privileged to identify with a church that runs several hundred of attendants in their various worship session. They had a committed old lady of 80yrs of age and have been there a number of years. This woman was spirit filled and dared to stay back at the altar groaning and praying in other tongues carrying the entire thing.

After some years of next visits to the church learnt that a new pastor came and saw the lady he learnt he doing the same thing at the altar and objected it before you know it, the number reduced drastically between attendants 30 to 35. When enquired of what happened to the attendance, by the visitor, he was told that the praying woman was stopped from doing what she was led by the spirit to be doing which has sustained the church growth without knowing by the new pastor.

In this chapter I want to look at several factors and perhaps a force believe to be capable of setting the course of any local church. Of course, the same factors can forward life and death to an entire network of churches and even to an organization. In Deuteronomy 30:15-20 God, through his servant Moses set life and death before Israel as a church. "So from this verse, we discover that God offered his people a choice

1. WHAT FIRES DEATH TO A CHURCH PRIDE:

This is a sin that can easily be fallen into especially if the church has experienced Gods great grace and favor. There is a tendency to think that we are special. This is wrong. We are part of every church. You and I are just as much an important part of the church down the road of our home church. We are not very special moreover, the only thing that makes us special is that we believe in

Jesus and even them it is by God's grace and Jesus sacrifice that enables us to believe and be saved.

2. DOCTRINAL DIVISION:

This is another factor that attracts death to a church. Every church needs to be in good biblical doctrine. Let me quickly make a distinction between essential and nonessential doctrines of our faith. The essential doctrines of our faith are the deity of Christ, the virgin birth, the death, burial and resurrection of Jesus, the Trinity, the Holy Spirit. And the Second coming of Jesus are the foundation pillars of Christianity. It is essential that we believe strongly on the above points or otherwise make mockery of your faith. But there are a whole of non-essential doctrines, based on our self-interpretation. Examples of the non-essential doctrines are Baptism of the Holy Spirit, eschatology, eternal security, ornaments, dress code, and use of cosmetics. To me, I want to say that they are collegial issues. The danger of this misconception of doctrines is that you may start your Christian fellowship on doctrine given by demons rather than that based on Jesus Christ. Again, there is nothing wrong in accepting the change when you know that your previous belief is erroneous.

3. FACTIONS AND DIVISIONS:

When these exist in the denomination, it attracts spiritual death. We can eve call it US verses THEM syndrome/mentality. One these factions develop, the door then opens wide for demonic forces to come in and form a scheme over the church. Actually, we need each other according to 1Cor 1212.17 which tells us that we are one body, No one member should consider himself any better than another Paul makes it crystal clear in his several admonitions. Another problem that grows out of these factions is that causes us to judge each other and this leads to fault finding strife and variance in the house of God. The scripture even tells us, if we see a fault in a brother, or sister, we should go out of our way to extend ourselves to that person. Show them the way out by love and encouragement, not by judging them. That is what a matured Christian person should do.

4. CONTROL

Excessive control or manipulation in a church will bring death to that body whether it is a rural or city church. This type of behavior usually crop up from the leader. But when the congregation know that it is not for the general interest of the church, may decide not to yield to such attitude.

Manipulation is another form of control but it is usually a little more subtle. Both are wrong no leader should allow himself to be tempted with such sins. They may work for a while, but eventually God will say "Enough is enough in some other places, some title members in the

Church will rise to resist the pastor in charge. This is an abomination and, it attracts a direct generational curse from God upon such group of persons.

5. SIN:

Sin in a church will cause it to die. But you may say Revd. Anoweh, does this make sense. Hence we all sin, yes, but the sin I talk about is that which permeates the church, and which most often has a stronghold on the leadership. These sins can be of sexual nature, gossip, greed, lying, etc. if, there are such sin permeating the body of Christ, the church will eventually experience death. God cannot allow such sin indefinitely either in an individual or in church at large.

Sin is as deadly as cancer. The word of God tells us that one's sin should find him out. The only thing that makes God to turn His a back church is sin. It was the same sin that warranted the expulsion of our old parents from the Garden of

Eden. When Jesus our Savior took the sins of the entire world, God overlooked him. So if God sees an in you no matter the level of relationship, he will remove his face entirely.

6. WRONG FOUNDATION: The last factor from this chapter that can expose the church to death is when the church has a faulty foundation. There is only one foundation. Any life-giving church that is built on a wrong foundation will grow only so strong and then it will decline. This is what happens to churches that are built on the person of General Overseer. It will only work for a while. Do you also think of what happens to such church if the person falls sick or dies? The best church is that which raise members abused on the personality of Jesus Christ. However, if the church must remain lively and benefit the society, the following factors should be considered paramount.

Consistently teach and abide in the word of God, The congregation must be thought biblical principles. It is not only teaching it but rather putting the word into practice.

A life giving church is always a praying church God is really calling His church into prayers never before. Prayer should be emphasized from the pulpit and demonstrated by the leader.

No church can really live without the fruits of the spirit permeating its members. The mentioned fruit includes the following.

Love, joy, peace, patience, kindness, goodness faithfulness and self-control. It is the fruit that gives peace to every member but today, the gift of the Holy Spirit is much emphasized. People now pursue the gift more than the fruits, itis absolutely wrong.

CHAPTER THIRTEEN

MY LOCAL CHURCH

Years ago a pastor who was not born again claimed so: He would only succeed to preach issue8 on jokes, poetry and social issues with very little scriptural base. His attending one international Ministers conference made him rebirthed. He came back to the same church and to make Jesus real to the people by preaching the crucified, died and resurrected Jesus. He noticed the impact when somebody woke up after service one day and controlled him that what he hears him preached is nothing but Jesus! Jesus!! and Jesus!!!. In this very chapter, we are going to examine the local church where you belong. Acts 2:42-47 gives us a vivid insight of how a local church should function. Revealed how the believers praised God, develop themselves in teaching, fellowship, prayer, gave to those in need when they sold their own possessions and ate together with glad and hearts. The result was that everyone was filled with awe, many signs and wonders were done by the apostles (church leaders) How exciting! These people were indeed in communion as they experienced the reality of Christ in every aspect of their lives. What is the actual meaning of church? Again as I said earlier, the church is not a building rather, it is one who is born-again with evidence accepting Jesus as His Lord and Savior. The actual word church literally means the called out one In original secular, it means "EKKLESSIA". The broader or universal church consists of every believer in Christ all over the world l includes all true born-again people of all living Christian denominations.

THE LOCAL CHURCH

This includes any group of believers who gather together to celebrate the goodness of the gospel. In the best sense. It is a true community of believer's committed to Christ and to each other. Christians should belong to a local church. It is in this church that we interact on the one-onone basis It is also within this context that we relate to other Christians, worship God, give our tithes and offerings while serving the Lord.

The same local church may or may not have it's own building where they meet. Years back when there were no building, Christians meet at convenient place, usually someone s house. The smallest church one can have is where we have two or three believers that seats together according to Matt 18:10.

THE FUNCTIONS OF THE DYNAMIC CHURCH

We can again, work with the real functions of the church in mind, irrespective of where it is situated. Each church is unique, there is no church on earth that is alike. Either should they function alike? Reason is that the operators are different people from different background. Moreover, there are certain identified functions that should be common to all churches. I am showcasing Jesus to the world. The most important duty of the church is to save the lost through evangelism. The church is the only qualified means on earth capable of preaching to the unsaved people of the world. This I mean can take place in various ways and carried out by church and individuals alike. Every church should have a progressive and well planned evangelism outfit to reach many places that people live. The following are suggested ways the local church can embark to spread the good news.

NEIGHBORHOOD BIBLE STUDY:

There should be a schedule bible studies in the homes of Christians where friends, relatives co-workers and neighbors can come to hear the word of God. This kind of atmosphere i8 welcoming and non-threatening to unbelievers, including those with strong non-Christians beliefs. This is a high effective way to reach the lost.

NEIGHBORHOOD CHILDREN'S FELLOWSHIP:

Research teaches us that over 80% of the people who become believers do so because they had a serious biblical parental upbringing. Therefore, it is very important to have active child evangelism modalities in our various local churches. Have a regular gathering of children meetings for game, refreshments, and storytelling. Which are all coined from the bible.

WITNESSING CLASSES:

One of the most important things to a believer is to learn how to lead someone to Christ. Periodical teaching how to witness to others about Christ should not be neglected.

OPEN AIR MEETINGS:

On regular basis, schedule open air meetings on vacant lots, parks, or lawns, etc.

Employ the service of contemporary Christian musicians and evangelists to speak. Sometimes several churches could come together to plan and sponsor a particular programmed with aim to win their environment to Christ..

2. PRAISEAND WORSHIP TO GOD:

The highest and primary call of God upon a church is to worship and praise him. Since Satan left that seat, it has remained vacant. God wants crop of people that will converge to worship and praise Him alone.

3 PRAYER:

The core business of the church is to pray, pray and then pray. We are actually familiar with Gods call to pray according to 2 Chron. 1:14 "nothing that comes from the mind of man can substitute for seeking the mind of Christ in prayer.

COMMUNION AND WATER BAPTISM:

These two are interrelated, every church should have periodical classes on water baptism and regularly schedule baptism services. And communion should be observed regularly in every local church. Some churches may have it on monthly or weekly basis.

CHAPTER FOURTEEN

CHURCH DISCIPLINE

In chapter 10 above, written based on Matthew chapter 18, we understand the degree of power the church receives. And as such, they should keep to it. The church of God on earth will really prosper if order and responsibility should be the principle.

In the world institution today, it is obvious that it is only in the military especially the ARMY that you will record absolute discipline. You are bound to obey the last order right from your recruitment. In fact it runs in the blood of every military person-a. As God is the God of order and if He lives in the house as He does in his church, that house must be according to His order. More so, since it is written holiness becometh thine house, oh Lord" (Ps 93:5), it is our responsibility to keep the assembly, His dwelling place, pure and holy. Even from where Mathews gospel chapter (12:13- 45) illustrates where the devil claims ownership of our bodies. And when he (the devil) comes back from where

he was cast out from, Seeing it clean and empty, he is bound to return and occupy. If devil is interested in convenience body then God should be more. This is an additional reason why our master Jesus died for those who made His house of prayer a thoroughfare.

We should not in the sense of populating the church condone

uncleanliness in the body of Christ that he ramsomly payed for.

Leaders of the churches should seat up and condemn out-rightly the devil that celebrates them in the church. We are very much afraid that when you discipline erring members, other churches will crown them as soon as they show up in their assembly. Beware, God loves righteousness and his biblical standard must be maintained.

GODS PURITY:

Discipline in the church is a necessity because God is the holy and true one (Rev 3:7) who is in the midst of His people and whose eyes are purer to behold evil or to look unto iniquity (Heb. 1:13). Sin cannot be allowed to go on unjudged or evil tolerated where the holy one has His habitation. His house must be kept clean. Psalm 101:7 declares: "he that worketh deceit shall not dwell within my house: he that tells lies shall not tarry in my sight".

It is important to remember as we take up the subject of discipline that it is connected with the aspect of the

church presented in the scripture the house of God. It is not the church as the body of Christ that is before us when considering the matter of discipline.

KEEP TO CHRIST AUTHORITY:

In book of Heb. 3:6we read of Christ being "son over his own house; whose house are we. Since Christ is son over his house, his authority must be maintained and the lawlessness of man shut out. What is agreeable to him is to be manifested. We have, therefore to act in the responsibility of maintaining the order of his words and to keep His house clean. This is the discipline of Christ as son over His house. It is ecclesiastical in chapter assembly discipline. The discipline of the father is that of fatherly care for a child. It is the exercise of individual love and grace flowing from the father's love towards an erring child. This is the father's care over his family and is quite distinct from the son exercising discipline over his house.

Discipline means subjected to rule, development of the habit of obedience by training and instruction, correction, and chastisement. It is the educative training of the disciple. This is what is necessary in the home, school, in government, and likewise in the house of God. No institution can prosper or succeed without some level of discipline.

If there is no maintenance of discipline and godly order in the a8sembly, it will soon be evident that the lack of it hinders the operation of the Holy Spirit and quenches His ministry. The spirit of God is grieved by all that dishonors Christ and that is contrary to his word. He cannot bless disobedience self-will, or unjudged sin. So spiritual death and lack of power in the assembly are sure to follow the neglect of discipline which should be exercised for the honor and glory of the Lord, whose house we are.

RUNNING CHARACTER OF SIN

Another reason for the necessity of discipline in the assembly is the fact that sin is like a leaven which leavens the whole lump. The apostles speak of this in 1 Corinthians 5:6-8. "Keep out therefore the old leaven, which ye may be a new lump, as ye are unleavened. The nature of leaven is such that even a small particle of it will spread, leavening effects is to purge it out or to bake it in an oven thus arresting its actions. Likewise sin will spread in an assembly and leaven the whole gathering if it is not judge and purged out. Sin is defiling. It must be judged whenever it manifests itself, otherwise it will become diffused and corrupt the whole company.

CONCLUSION

The church from the chapters has been said to me an (biblically) or referred to as "people and not a place building or cathedral. The church is an institution built and established by God with love, kindness mercy, grace, humility, Joy, peace, unity, etc as it pillars. This is to say that, the church can only stand firm if all mentioned above are applied in our day-in. day-out routine.

Guiding the existence of the church (God's people) is the desire of Christ to love us unconditionally and give us his ever satisfying and unlimited salvation through accepting him as our personal Lord and Savior. God's wish is for us to draw nearer to him, (by being punctual at church services despite religious differences in the society), and gain eternal dinning with him. Also, God wants us to realize that how we think and behave leaves indelible mark on the totality of our well-being. That is, he is indirectly telling us not to think of the church as any kind of building. God is in fact, the church himself, so why refer to it as an ordinary cathedral?

It is pertinent to note that such tendencies as propelled by Matthew and Timothy in the bible where the title of this piece of writing were drawn has to be taken serious. Because neglecting it could give rise to the derailing of moral values both in the church and in the world. And in considerations of the above, moral

ineptitude could be identified as the fundamental fall outs of many Christian who chose to contravene orders rather than abide he above them. Also, the breakdown of morality would be religious problem because it will indirectly question the old age of our Christian orientation, thereby putting our "holier than thou" attitude in jeopardy.

Furthermore, obvious sinful act should be avoided and neglected. Because sin, no matter the level, makes us wander far away from God and things He can offer us. A sinner has nothing to do with God and his prayers are an abomination in His sight. We should be desirous of leaving our imprint in the church and also endeavor, as ladies to marry as virgin so that one day; if not you or your husband boast about it, God will. We should also be ambitious in exhibiting some of these rewarding acts and make it a clear manifestation of the nature of the 21" century- in Christ personality and not otherwise. We should know that we are in Christ and Christ is in us too. Have we not had enough already? Aren't we tired of our old and sinful way of living? How will you feel when God directly tells you that you are not living up to His expectation?

This book no doubt identifies the major problems encountered by Christians due to the ignorance and therefore outlines ways of resolving them. It points out the inadequacies, and joins in the litany of voices lamenting on the derailing moral values in the CHURCH and their lackadaisical attitude towards the works of God. By doing this, it makes the church a more sustainable and understandable institution.

BIBLIOGRAPHY

Dr. M. Dewane Anderson(2014) Growth In The knowledge of the Lord cooper Abraham the ii (1973)

An International Minister's Manual Jim and Carolyn Murphy. Printed Malasha Hundred fold press P.O. Box 420178 R.K campbell the Church of the living God. (1990) believing bookshelf Inc. Canada. Uche Christian Benjamin 2011 the Beauty of A Christian. Breakthrough publication 136 Cameroon Rd. Aba.

Kola Onalapo, Church growth (2009) unusual publishers, Lagos. Kola Onalapo, seven reasons for marriage

delays(2005) Raph Mahonuy (1968) Victorious Christian Living, World Missionary Assistance Plan Goon Glenoaks Buibank, CA 91502 USA.

Oxford Advanced Learners Dictionary. Wikipedia word dictionary. Www.web MD RKC Campbell (1990). The church of the living God. Believers bookshelf Inc, Cannada.

ACKNOWLEDGMENT

I appreciated he immeasurable contributions received from my son in the Lord Dr Obinnali Ifeanyi, who spent time to contribute in the editing of the work. Also my youngest son Winner for his consistency in typing of this work. God bless Hon. Joe Mankpa for his courage and advice in the course of this work. I acknowledge the members of my church and my father in the Lord, the Prime Bishop of Holiness Evangelistic Church Bishop (Dr.) Chima Amadi for his spiritual impact in my life and ministry. Also Engr. Edward my Sunday school coordinator whose contribution to this work was immense; also Divine Nwaneri and Pastor Uche Nnawuihe, who were readily available to meet the demands at each stage of this publication.

I also wish to make mention of a great friend, Prof. Mrs Blessing ljeoma and my family friend Rev. G. Okoro for their financial contributions.

Finally, I give everlasting heartful appreciation to my humble and loving wife Mrs. Victoria for her moral and spiritual contributions towards the production of this book.

www.ingramcontent.com/pod-product-compliance
Lightning Source LLC
LaVergne TN
LVHW052056160826
845678LV00015B/3259

9798351773346